If It's Going To BE…

IT'S UP TO ME!

The Beginner's Guide To

Self-Discovery

By Mike T. Lightner

Chief Master Sergeant (Retired), US Air Force

Alaska

IT'S UP TO ME!

Printed in the United States of America

First Printing, 2018

ISBN-13: 978-0999657010
ISBN-10: 0999657011

Dare2Dream LD Productions
dare2dreamleadership@gmail.com

www.d2dleadership.com

CONTENTS

INTRODUCTION

Before I get started, I think it's important that I share a little bit about my background. If you have already read my book, *Lead Bold – Lead Strong – Lead Well: 9 Proven Leadership Secrets Anyone Can Learn and Apply,* you have probably already read much of this and can skip ahead to the next section. However, for those of you who haven't yet read my other book, I'll give you the short version here.

I was born in a small farm town in Northern Illinois called Belvidere. I was blessed with two wonderful parents, Paul and Joyce Lightner, and seven brothers and sisters. Now, being the youngest of eight kids growing up, my focus honestly was to get out of the house as quickly as I could. Because of this, my decision to enlist in the Air Force wasn't a surprise to anyone.

In fact, I had decided when I was ten years old I was going into the Air Force. My dream was to be a pilot. Not just any pilot, I was going to be a pilot in their premier aerial demonstration squadron, the Thunderbirds. Unfortunately, in Elementary School, I was told I had a reading disability and from that point on I believed that I simply wasn't smart enough to ever make this dream become a reality. So, at the age of 17, I settled for whatever the Air Force would give me. I enlisted in the United States Air Force in December of 1985 and in June of 1986, shortly after graduating high school, I was on my way to basic training.

Like a lot of Airmen in the early years of service, I struggled. Lucky for me, under the mentorship of my supervisor, Steve Nitahara, I was able to overcome many of these challenges. However, based on feedback I had received during my early school years, I never really expected to amount to anything. In fact, looking back there were probably many self-destructive things I did to make sure that this negative image I had of myself remained true. It would take me many years of failure and self-discovery to find out this "mental model of failure" I had built for myself simply wasn't true...I was capable of much more and If It's Going To BE...if I were going to break the cycle of self-destruction...IT'S UP TO ME!

To read or hear someone say "If It's Going To BE...IT'S UP TO ME!" almost seems to simple. But consider this: I went from nearly failing out of high school, struggling and nearly getting fired as a mid-level supervisor, to being promoted to the highest enlisted rank in the Air Force and graduating college in the top 1% of my class and the only thing that really changed…was me!

The truth of the matter is, I had always had the potential inside me…I just lacked the belief in myself and the knowledge and understanding of a few basic principles. These principles are something you can learn and apply too. Perhaps the best part is…you don't need to go through 20 years of failure and self-discovery to learn, understand, and apply them in your life. I have gathered them for you, right here in this book.

IT'S UP TO ME!

To my brother Philip A. Lightner.

Your life will not be measured by the years you spent with us.

But by the impact you made and continue to make long after you're gone.

I love and miss you!

IT'S UP TO ME!

ACKNOWLEDGMENTS

I have to say a huge thank you to all the marvelous minds whose work has contributed to my own growth over the years and consequently ended up in this book in different forms.

And huge heart felt thank you to my Mother, Joyce M. Lightner, for always believing in me...even when I was struggling to believe in myself. When it comes to Moms, I drew the winning ticket in the lottery of life. My Mom is one in a Billion and has always been my number one supporter, regardless of how crazy my dreams were. She was there to celebrate through the wins and provide comfort when things didn't turn out as planned. From my earliest memories, my Mom was a role model, working hard in the factory all day and still finding the time to love and care of us kids when she returned home. Mom, I love you!

IT'S UP TO ME!

CHAPTER 1

You Can Do Better!

"The secret of change is to focus all of your energy, not on fighting the old, but on building the new."

~ Socrates

A few years ago, my friend and mentor Roddy Galbraith shared with me a wonderful story about his son and an apple seed. As I thought about all the different ways I could start this book, I quickly realized this would be the perfect story to share with you.

My seven-year-old son Leon had cut his apple up and as usual left the plate, the knife and the discarded apple core on the side. I'm not sure when, but at some point one of our four children had picked out all the apple seeds and left them on the table. They were moved around, pushed and dragged by various bits of paper until the cleaners got sick of moving them and eventually threw them away. All except one. One had fallen to the floor, escaping detection!

For days that little apple seed was kicked around on the wooden floor. It eventually fell into a gap between two floorboards and remained there for some time.

Weeks later Leon rediscovered it and announced, "I'm going to plant this seed and grow an apple tree!" Not wanting to extinguish his enthusiasm, I didn't tell him that this little apple seed was dead. We wrapped it between two damp paper towels and placed it in a dark cupboard, like he had learned at school.

He was both delighted and amazed when the little seed sprouted in just a few days! His attention span, being typical of most seven-year-old boys, meant that within a minute of first witnessing his seed's heroic struggle for life, he was off playing his favorite video game.

I sat and thought about that seed for some time though. While it was on the hard, dry kitchen floor it was helpless. It would never grow into anything. It would never DO anything. It would just sit there.

But what really caught my attention was the fact that as soon as it was placed into an environment that was more conducive to its growth, it burst into life. It wasn't dead after all. The potential was obviously there all along, but you would have never known it to see it squashed in the gap of the floor.

Today that seedling has been moved into a little pot with some earth and is growing into an apple tree, just like Leon said at the beginning.

Isn't that a wonderful story? It is very natural for the seed to germinate and sprout. It's very natural for the seedling to grow into a little tree. And it's very natural for the tree to reach for the sky and grow as big as it possibly can. It doesn't take effort to grow. It does it because of what it is – a tree!

The seed may well have been more comfortable sitting on the floor with nothing to do, but that's not what trees are supposed to do, is it? They're supposed to grow. And they're supposed to keep growing until they stop growing. And when they stop growing they die.

As I look back at my life, I realize that all too often I've been far too much like the seed, lying on the warm floor, than the seedling in the pot! Not so much in later life, but certainly for vast stretches of my earlier life. If I was comfortable, I didn't want to move!

The trouble with this mindset is that no one else is going to move you. We all have to paddle our own canoe. If you sit back and rest, then by default you'll begin to drift along with the flow instead of where you actually want to go. And water only ever flows downhill!

A few years back, at a certification event I was attending, I heard my friend and mentor, John Maxwell, say that everything worth having is uphill. And I think that most of us can recognize and accept that when we stop and think about it. When we're comfortable, we don't spend too much time thinking about what we want, where it is or how we can get it. Instead, we focus on what we don't want and worry about losing what we have.

In Roddy's story, Leon's little tree has a very clear goal, to reach for the light. And this goal is pursued relentlessly every single day of its life. Little wonder it makes such great progress.

If we all had such clear objectives and pursued them continually, I'm sure we would astound ourselves with what we are capable of.

Why don't more people make such great progress in their lives then, I wonder? The statistics are staggeringly disappointing when you look at them. Only 5% of people ever reach financial independence. I read once that most people die within seven years of retiring. Almost everyone is unhappy in their job and nearly everyone argues about money!

Is this all we have to look forward to after a lifetime of experience? What happened to all those hopes and dreams we shared so freely as a child? Where did that hope and wonder of the world go? What happened to that daily happiness that seemed to ooze out of us, infecting everyone around us? Why is true happiness so evasive for so many and what do we have to do to get more of it?

Perhaps happiness is a childish fantasy, something that is not meant for grownups! As I sit here thinking about Leon's little sapling, is it as happy as a toddler, I wonder? Will it stop being happy when it reaches a certain size and then become a miserable, pessimistic, know-it-all adult; only to finally become a gnarled, cantankerous old apple tree?

In John Maxwell's great book, *The 15 Invaluable Laws of Growth*, he tells a story that I just love. As the fortune teller reads the man's fortune she says, "You'll be poor and miserable until you are 40 years old." "Then what happens?" asks the man with a glint of hope. "Then you get used to it!"

I love the prophetic brilliance in that story – not for everyone of course, but for many people. It is sad but oh so true, isn't it?

Thucydides said, "The secret to happiness is freedom. And the secret to freedom is courage." Surely this applies to individuals just as much as it applies to nations, races or communities. How many people do you know who have the courage to pursue flexibility and freedom in their lives in an appropriate way, and do you think they are happy?

Another great source of guidance for billions of people around the world says, "Straight is the gate and narrow is the way and few there be that find it." Could that mean peace and happiness is indeed a scarce thing?

A great mentor of mine said that happiness is an inside job. It's not something you get from external circumstances or things. It is the result of what's going on inside. He said that there is almost a 100% correlation between happiness and awareness or levels of consciousness. The more aware person can be happy almost completely detached from externals while the unaware person is unhappy almost no matter what. Nothing you can do for them will make them happy.

Perhaps happiness is, as Earl Nightingale said, "the progressive realization of a worthy ideal."

If Leon's little tree were capable of experiencing happiness in a tree-like way, I think it would be happiest when it was reaching and stretching and growing for the light – a worthy ideal, slowly but unstoppably realized, in ever-greater degrees but never completed.

Do you have a philosophy on life and happiness? How committed are you to this belief? Is it realistic? Is it logical? And most importantly of all, is it helping you?

Whatever your philosophy on happiness, taking responsibility for your growth, having the courage to face life and get the best out of whatever experiences you face is undoubtedly the best strategy for growth for every aspect of your nature.

I hope in some small way this book can help you in that pursuit by giving you a formula for extracting more of the rich marrow out of life.

It works for everyone that works it and applies it.

Life is a wonderful adventure. You are already very good at it, but you can get better. Every effort you make to develop and grow through your life experiences will inevitably be reflected in your experience of the world.

It certainly is true that we all get experience, but not all of us stop and think about what we can learn from these experiences. All too often we carry on banging our head against the same wall without realizing it is of our own making, and not only do we not have to bang our head against it, but it's not actually there at all.

Wherever you are on your journey, whatever the circumstances of your life and however you feel about it all at the moment of reading these words, I want to reach out to you and let you know that you are a wonderful human being capable of far more than you ever thought possible. You have more potential than you can ever dream of using. You are perfectly imperfect, just like everyone else. You are no better than anyone else and no worse. You are doing great, but you can do better!

...And you should!

"All I ask is the chance to prove that money won't make me happy."

~ Spike Milligan

ACTION EXERCISES

What would a dream life look like for you?

If you knew you couldn't fail, what would you go after?

If you were to leave this world right now, would you be content with what you've done here and who you've become?

When it's all over and someone is summing up your life and the kind of person you are, what do you think they would say?

What would you like them to say?

Write out the answers, or think about them, or better yet, discuss them with a loved one.

IT'S UP TO ME!

CHAPTER 2

WHERE ARE YOU STUCK?

"If the highest aim of a captain were to preserve his ship, he would keep it in port forever."

~ Thomas Aquinas

Growing up my Dad was a major baseball fan. In fact, if the Cubs were playing everything in our house would stop until the game was over. So it was only natural when I was old enough to play, he would encourage me to get onto a team.

It didn't take long before I started to discover my love for the game as well. Not so much for the game itself but for the training and physical activity. I just loved to be active. However, by the time I reached middle school my love of baseball had faded and I decided to try my hand at other sports.

For two years in middle school, I tried out for the basketball team and wasn't selected either year. This probably had to do with the fact that I was way to short but in the end that was ok because I couldn't touch a basketball without jamming a finger. I had to face it, basketball just wasn't my thing.

However, during one of my eighth grade gym classes our teacher introduced us to wrestling and boy was I hooked...I knew what I was going to do next...I was going to be a wrestler.

During my freshman year of High School I tried out and made the school's wrestling team. I worked out relentlessly, gaining 35 pounds between my freshman and sophomore years. I wasn't that good but that didn't matter, I didn't care that I lost, only that I did better than the match before. My love for working out and wrestling continued nearly all the way through High School until I discovered the thrill of racing motorcycles, well dirt bikes more specifically.

Although I never raced dirt bikes professionally, I loved how physically demanding the sport was and would race against my friends every chance I could. This continued on after I graduated from High School and enlisted into the United States Air Force.

Then one day, everything changed, I crashed my dirt bike in the woods and was thrown into some trees. After 8 hours of surgery and 28 days in the hospital, I was finally able to walk again but only with the help of crutches and a stiff leg in brace.

Weeks later, when the brace was finally removed, I was amazed at how small my left leg had become. In full transparency, I honestly didn't think much of it at the time, I was just happy to be walking again.

After months of physical therapy, things just didn't seem to be getting any better. I could walk but I had a bad limp that just didn't seem to be going away.

Finally, I went to a specialist and he told me there was nothing wrong with my leg!

An interesting thing had happened. Apparently, my brain had subconsciously decided to rest the muscles in my leg. I said I was going to rest it and my body complied. For months on end I had not been using the muscles in my left leg as normal. The specialist noticed this right away. "Look in the mirror at the difference between your left leg and your right." I couldn't believe I hadn't noticed how bad it had gotten. My left leg was literally half the size of the right!

The confirmation from a man in a white coat that there was nothing really wrong with it, and that it was more psychological than physical, gradually led me to being able to operate normally again, although the whole process ended up being a three or four-year journey!

I realize now that I've learned much more in life from my injuries than my health, and that particular injury really hammered home the principle "use it or lose it!" We are designed to use our marvelous bodies, not to continually seek out inactivity because it's comfortable.

It is true for us and all other life, isn't it? We are designed for continual growth in all areas of our lives and all areas of our personality – body, mind and spirit.

And if we are not growing in a particular area of life, if we are not getting better, then we are getting worse! Nothing stands still. Everything is moving in one direction or the other. It is either going forward or backward. It is in a state of growth or a state of disintegration.

Everything is perpetually changing. Our world around us today is changing at a faster rate than ever before. The only way we can be comfortable in such a world is to learn to learn. We need to be able to constantly adapt and grow. We need to constantly be able to learn, unlearn and relearn!

I remember hearing a story once of a speaker opening a presentation by walking on stage with a six-foot tall dinosaur. He set it down on the stage, and then wrote RTC in big letters on the flip chart. He then took a live white mouse out of his briefcase and let it run from hand to hand for about 30 seconds. Looking up at the audience he asked, "Who would have put money on this little guy outlasting this big guy sixty-five million years ago? Then he turned to the board and said, "Resistant To Change!"

I have studied and taught professional speaking for years, but I've never come across another opener like that! It makes a great point, doesn't it?

We are adaptive beings. We can assess and learn from our environments and change to fit them more optimally. In fact, adapting like this is more than just change.

I recently read that change is a different way of doing, whereas transformation is a different way of being. And evolution is perpetual transformation.

To thrive for sustained periods of time we need to be in a state of continual evolution.

This is difficult to do though, certainly for many people. We don't like change, do we? As Tom Feltenstein said, "Change is good...You go first!".

"The problem with the world is the intelligent people are full of doubts and the stupid people are full of confidence."

~Charles Bukowski

ACTION EXERCISES

Where are you stuck in your life?

Which particular fears are holding you back?

Are there things you want, that you are not going after?

When was the last time you did something you've never done before?

Write out the answers, or think about them, or better yet, discuss them with a loved one.

IT'S UP TO ME!

CHAPTER 3

WHO IS GOING TO DO IT FOR YOU?

"Responsibility is the price of freedom."

~ Elbert Hubbard

It's funny how we have a feeling of invincibility when we're young, isn't it? I used to do all kinds of self-destructive things and I never gave a thought to the impact it had on my health. Now I feel bad if I don't pull the skin off my chicken properly!

I remember, after joining the Air Force, arriving at my first duty station. I was young but still a drinker and would hang out at the squadron bar on Friday nights. Often times I would stand there chatting with the other drinkers and share a joke or two with an eclectic cross section of the squadron's personnel. Same faces nearly every Friday, from the First Sargent and orderly room staff to the pilots and even sometimes the Commander. I remember Scotty came up to talk to me while I was asking one of the pilots about flying. As we walked back to our work center, Scotty said, "How do you know so many people, I don't know that many and I've been here three years longer."

It was an interesting thought that the drinking club had a certain solidarity. Several years later I remembered this when my son was born and I gave up drinking...well the hard stuff anyways.

My relationship with the other drinkers in my social club, and one in particular who I had worked closely with, changed forever the moment I left the club.

It is a peculiar realization indeed when you begin to change and grow that the people around you, many of whom you love and who love you, don't like it!

As we discussed in the last chapter, no one really likes change. Particularly change that happens to you, as opposed to change that you choose and drive yourself.

There's a certain dynamic to any club or group and the homeostasis is maintained by everyone doing and being the same. If someone goes and changes, it ruins it for everyone else!

This is especially true of a "negative" type group – smoking, partying and irresponsible behavior, drug use, etc. If you change your life and stop going to the club every weekend you are, in essence, reminding your friends at the club that maybe they really shouldn't be living like this anymore. Worse yet, you're saying that you have the courage to change and they don't. Now things are awkward and they have a decision to make. They have to justify their choice to stay right where they are, and very often they do this by bashing you and your noble attempt at a better life!

"Who do you think you are anyway? So, you're better than us now?"

In our drinking group, one of the people remaining in the group said he had spoken to his doctor about quitting and his doctor had advised against it. He actually told us his doctor recommended that he carry on drinking! How can you deceive yourself to that extent?

Very easily.

We don't like change. And we don't like feeling bad about ourselves, so we will go to ridiculous extents to justify our thoughts, feelings and actions.

What does this mean for our quest for success? It means that if you are going to change then you have to be ready for everything to change. Don't worry, it's a good thing, but being aware in advance is the antidote you need, because it hurts when people don't do what you expect them to.

If you think about this, it means that people you love as well as those you are indifferent about, will try and keep you stuck where you are, consciously or often unconsciously, because they don't understand or they don't want change to happen to them.

Put another way, it means that when you decide that you want something, you need to overcome the gravitational pull of everyone in your environment because they don't want you to have it! I know that sounds crazy, but it is true. It's not that you can't get them on board, often you can, but you need to grow and take them with you, not expect them to help you get there.

And some of them will accept the new you, but many will not.

Everyone in your life has some kind of vested unconscious desire for you to carry on as you are, so if you want change, no one is going to do it for you. We all have to take complete and utter responsibility for ourselves. Expecting others to do it for us, or even to be on board with us, just sets us up for disappointment.

This presents many problems for well-meaning parents, doesn't it? My parents and I have many conversations about spoiling the children and the constant evaluation of whether we're neglecting them or empowering them.

I remember a time when I was 16, out driving around with some guy friends and some girls we knew from school. There were six of us in the car, three boys in the front and three girls in the back. As the only one old enough to have a driver's license, I was trying to show off and was driving too fast for the road conditions. It was the middle of winter in Illinois and the roads were covered with snow and ice. But I was ready for whatever the streets would throw at me or so I thought.

As I was speeding past other cars, we came across a set of railroad tracks. These tracks had just enough of a bump to cause the rear wheels to lose traction. As the car swerved back and forth, I fought to keep it on the road and from hitting other cars. Within a few seconds, the car was rear end first into a large ditch full of snow. In a few exhausting seconds our light hearts and hopes had turned to disaster, my arrogance turned to respect and humility.

We were miles from our homes and no idea how we were going to get ourselves out of the situation. The girls took it upon themselves to walk up to the road and hitch a ride with the first car that would stop. Leaving us boys to figure it out on our own.

As we stood there staring at the car, my mind raced for answers. How were we going to get out of this mess? I vividly remember the overwhelming feeling I had to call my dad and ask him what we should do. It wasn't a thought, it was an emotion —a powerful emotional pull. And I don't know why, but I also recognized that it was time for me to take responsibility for this and to sort it out myself. I also realized at that moment that I had depended on my parents for far, far too long…and that had to change!

Taking responsibility is the first step of many different systems of help and change. For as long as you believe that someone or something else is responsible for your growth, nothing is going to change. The world will continue to hold up the same merciless mirror, reflecting back the same life experience until you accept responsibility and agree to take the helm and chart your own course.

If you are not living the life you dream of, and most people aren't, it's not your mom or dad's fault, nor your spouse, your children, the government, the economy, the weather or anything or anyone else's.

We have all been gifted with the ability to choose what to do in any and every moment. Different choices take us in different directions. But with that marvelous gift of free will comes the responsibility for the decisions we make. In many ways it's as simple as that!

Years ago, while working at the Pentagon, I used to commute into the city of Washington DC on the bus. It was 30 minutes each way of looking at all the sad faces – same faces nearly every day. Same seats nearly every day! One day, as I was traveling, a video I had seen on TV popped into my head. In it, cattle was being rounded up and pushed through these large metal gates where they were then pushed two by two into this large train car so they could be taken off to market.

When I was telling a colleague at work of my amusing thought, Einstein's quote leapt out at me and smacked me over the head, "Insanity is doing the same things over and over again expecting different results."

I'm sure some of the half million people who commute into Washington DC every single day are very happy and grateful for the opportunity. But I'm equally certain that many dream of a bigger, better life. I wonder how many of them will wait until someone does it for them?

Guess how long they'll be waiting? A very long time.

"You take your life in your own hands and what happens?   A terrible thing, no one to blame!"

~ Erica Jong

ACTION EXERCISES

Who do you depend on in your life?

What do you depend on them for?

Are there important things in your life that you are waiting for other people do deliver?

What would it take for you to do what you are waiting for them to do?

Write out the answers, or think about them, or better yet, discuss them with a loved one.

IT'S UP TO ME!

CHAPTER 4

WHAT IS IT YOU WANT, I MEAN REALLY?

"Goals that are casually set are freely abandoned at the first obstacle."

~ Zig Ziglar

As I started putting together this chapter, I quickly realized I just had to use another story from my friend and mentor Roddy Galbraith. As a professional speaking coach, Roddy has hundreds if not thousands of amazing stories but this one about his wonderful wife Susan and their son Leon is absolutely priceless.

About five years ago, in early December, Susan came back to the family home with our son, Leon who was about three at the time. Everyone was out and she had forgotten her house keys. Standing outside in the cold she pondered how she could get in.

Our house has a large mailbox that you can fit a small package through and she thought that Leon just might be able to squeeze through it. So she said, "Leon, if I push you through the letter box, can you go into the kitchen, get a chair, stand on it, reach Mummy's keys and pass them back to me through the letter box?"

Leon, of course replied, "I'd love to!"

And so in he went. He just squeezed through, and except for the two large Rhodesian ridgeback dogs on the other side furiously licking his head until he got through, he made it in unharmed.

Susan directed him saying, "Go and get the chair now Leon and bring it back."

Leon went off, and Susan could hear a great deal of noise as the chair dragged across the floor. Then she could hear more noises and dragging as Leon struggled with the chair. Eventually he came back and said, "I can't do it! It's stuck."

Not wanting him to give up, Susan asked, "What's it stuck on?"

Leon replied, "The door."

Okay, she knew an 18-inch wide chair could easily make it through a 30-inch wide doorway! So Susan said, "Leon it's really important. Please try and have another go."

So Leon went off for another try. There was more noise, and then it went quiet. Susan waited for a minute or two then started to panic a little bit. She shouted through the letter box for an update. None came.

After a few more minutes she ran around to the kitchen window and peered in. She could see Leon, and thankfully he was ok. He was sitting on the floor in the middle of the kitchen. As she looked she could see that he was eating. Then she saw the back of the chair. It was next to the cupboard in the kitchen.

Apparently, Leon had given up on his assignment and instead, dragged the chair back into the kitchen. He had put it up against the cupboard, climbed up onto it and stood on his tiptoes to unhook his sister's Advent calendar off the wall. There he was, sitting on the floor eating all the chocolates out of it!

When I first heard this story I laughed so hard, for so long, I nearly peed myself. As I've thought about it since then, I've realized it highlights a really important aspect of human nature. When it comes to someone else's goals, almost anything is too much trouble, or too difficult or inconvenient. But when it comes to our own goals, things that we really want, there is almost no limit to the risks we'll take, the energy we will invest, and the creativity we can draw upon to satisfy our hearts' desires.

When we are locked onto a goal that's important to us, everything in life is simpler.

Decision making is easy. Priorities are sorted in a heartbeat. Distractions don't stand a chance.

What is it that you want? What will stimulate your very best thinking today? What will cause you to launch and push onward, even if you haven't had your coffee yet?

There's an old saying, "No one washes a rental car!" It's true, isn't it? If you don't own it, you just don't feel the same way about it. Don't let anyone else dictate your goals for you. You must find things that you want to go after! You are worth it. You deserve it, and as you progressively grow to the point where you achieve your goals and dreams, you will attain more of that seemingly elusive thing called happiness.

Earl Nightingale said, "Happiness is the progressive realization of a worthy ideal."

It is a funny thing that most people never really think about. What it is they want? I mean really want. They will list off the things that they don't want very quickly, but seem to get stuck with what they do want.

Paul Martinelli often says, "Most people say they want a lot more than they actually do and they settle for far less than they could easily get."

What are some of the things you truly want? Give yourself permission to stop and think about this question. Don't include the things you need. There is far less motivational drive involved with needs. I want you to think of the things that ignite your passion —the things that give you that surge of energy and a feeling of purpose. These are your worthy goals and dreams, and I've got good news for you concerning them. You don't have to settle for a life that excludes them. You just have to pinpoint what they actually are.

I think one of the main benefits of being really clear on this is that the desire to achieve or attain something really pulls us forward. It tempts us into growth. Going after something we don't actually know how to achieve (because we haven't paved the way yet) forces us to tackle new situations and challenges in order to continue the process of growth in our lives. It forces us to take advantage of opportunities that we, perhaps, didn't even see before, or discounted as being too risky.

Going after something we want forces us to pick ourselves up after things go wrong and to try something else.

Indifference does none of these things.

The things that we want can be large or small. They can take a few hours to achieve or a lifetime. The bigger the goal and the longer it takes to achieve, the more order it introduces into our lives.

Order is heaven's first law.

For us to achieve anything meaningful, we need order and movement. One without the other doesn't really work, does it?

In James Allen's great book, *As a Man Thinketh*, there is a chapter about thought and purpose. At the beginning of this chapter, he reminds us, "Until thought is linked with purpose, there is no intelligent accomplishment."

So the order that comes from a clear objective permeates every aspect of our life. Order to our thinking. Order to our actions. And order to our results.

When I talk to people about this, most of them can quickly see that order comes from a clear direction, objective or compass bearing. What they truly struggle with though is the answer to life's greatest question, "What is my purpose?"

Peter Drucker said something marvelous to assist with the answer, "Only musicians, mathematicians and a few early maturing people, their numbers limited, know what they want to do from an early age. The rest of us have to find out."

As you embark upon this journey of "finding out" your life purpose, you're going to have to push past a lot of things that hold most people back from this journey.

Fear will try to creep in and tell you, "Oh, those are just pipe-dreams. You need to be grateful for what you have. Not everyone is marked for greatness. Just stay where you are. Do what has the least amount of risk." Essentially, all of these fear-based thoughts are attempting to convince you to settle for a life that is far less than you are capable of being. Is that what you want? Of course not.

Then you're going to have to learn to face your fears. They will always be there. They'll be waiting for your weakest moments so they can swoop in and tell you to give up. But when you're willing to pull the mask off of fear, you'll see that all the things you are tempted to worry about are ridiculous.

Yes, you might fall down. You might look foolish. You might make a huge mistake. But the other side of that looks like this:

- You'll get back up.

- You'll learn from mistakes.

- You'll become an inspiration to others.

To me, that's worth the trials, the mistakes, the obstacles and even the temporary foolish moment.

Peter Drucker also said, "People who don't take risks generally make about two big mistakes a year. People who do take risks make about two big mistakes a year."

I'd rather make my mistakes actively engaging in the pursuit of my goals and dreams. How about you?

> *"The problem with quoting people off the Internet is you can never actually be sure they said it."*
>
> ~ Abraham Lincoln

ACTION EXERCISES

When was the last time you sat down and listed all the things you want?

What are the five most important things you would like to achieve?

Which areas of your life are you really content with?

Which areas of your life are you not content with?

Write out the answers, or think about them, or better yet, discuss them with a loved one.

IT'S UP TO ME!

CHAPTER 5

WHAT IS REAL, THE DANGER OR THE FEAR?

"We cannot live better than in seeking to be become better."

~ Socrates

I once heard from a friend who was studying Cognitive Behavioral Hypnotherapy, at the London College of Clinical Hypnosis, babies are born with just two fear responses, a fear response to loud noises and a fear response to the threat of falling. Clearly my son, Tristin, was not part of this study because he defiantly didn't fear falling. At least, not until he was a little older and broke his arm jumping off a slide.

With my son being the exception, the idea that we are born with just two fears is very interesting to me and provides a great deal of hope for the future of anyone who has suffered any kind of trauma that gets in the way of living their life and achieving the things they want to achieve.

The developmental stages and the fears the children learn as they develop are also very interesting.

At around eight to ten months, babies begin to understand "object permanence". Before this point, if something is in their awareness it exists. When it is removed from their awareness it ceases to exist. But after this stage, the idea that something is still in existence but just not there at that moment occurs. This leads to other trains of thought, like, "Where has Mom gone? When will she be back?" This is connected to separation anxiety.

I was in the Air Force most of Tristin's life. When he was two years old I had to go to a conference related to my work so my Mom flew up to take care of him. Tristin loved his Grandma and was happy, calm, and never really asked where Daddy was in the normal course of the first day. On day two of my trip, however, Tristin asked where Daddy was. This progressed to Tristin asking where Daddy was several times a day for the remainder of my trip.

When I returned, Tristin immediately latched onto me and has never let me go! Our relationship was forever changed after that trip.

One of the other key developmental stages for children occurs with the development of the imagination. Every parent notices a difference in the play of their child if they pay attention. They start making stuff up. They start lying! What is interesting about this stage is that fears can then come from sources that can't be seen. Enter bogey men and things that go bump in the night!

My son will probably kill me when he reads this but I just have to share. When Tristin was three, he had seen something on the TV that spooked him. I don't remember what it was but that night when he went to bed, he must have called me into his room at least a dozen times. "Daddy, I need a drink" "Daddy, can you read to me?" "Daddy, there is something under my bed." "Daddy..." You get the point. That night, I ended up just giving up and sleeping in his room. The next few nights were basically the same and I knew something had to change. Then entered Carmelo. Carmelo was a little stuffed bear, but don't let her cuteness fool you, she was a trained monster hunter. If there were any monsters in the house, Carmelo would sniff them out and eat them! From that night on, Tristin slept soundly, Carmelo squeezed tightly in his arms.

It is a normal part of children's development to go through these different stages of fear. What is important is that they are transitory. As children learn to overcome these fears they learn that they can deal with life, they can overcome challenges and say to themselves, "That wasn't so bad after all!"

As adults though, if we are stuck with a certain irrational fear, it may or may not be a problem. If it is stopping us from getting what we want, then maybe it is a problem to be worked on and overcome.

It's an interesting thing about fear; we put total faith in it. We feel that something is going to happen and we then trust that implicitly. We allow it to control our thinking, our feeling and our actions…and therefore our results.

Perhaps this is what Roosevelt was talking about in his inaugural address when he said, "The only thing we have to fear is fear itself."

If you think about it, it's interesting because the fear we experience doesn't exist anywhere in the entire universe except inside of us. You can't point to it anywhere in the world other than the feelings, thinking and actions, and sometimes even the symptoms you experience in your body.

So does that mean the fear isn't real? If two people face the same situation, one feels fear and the other doesn't, does that mean that one of them is making it up?

The fear is not to be confused with the danger. Make no mistake, danger is real. Busy roads are dangerous and cars can kill you. They can kill you if you step out into the road. If you are in the road and there is a car coming for you, you should get out of the way quickly! In the right situation, panic can even be a very appropriate emotion. But that's very different from sitting safely in your house panicking because of the cars out on the road. Experiencing a fear of cars when you are safe inside is an irrational fear. It's not real.

It sounds like a silly statement, but that's what we do when we fear the fear. A healthy concern, sensible caution, a few basic safety procedures and there is no need for the emotional response at all. Why use it then? Because we've learned to use it and now the tail is wagging the dog!

If you think about it, if fear is successful in its objective, you avoid the situation you fear and never actually know if the fear was founded in the first place. And because you always experience the fear, you never find out what would happen if you just exercised basic caution without the emotion. The emotion will convince you of its necessity and if you comply, you'll never know any different. Every time you engage avoidance because of fear, you are reinforcing the credibility of the fear.

The interesting thing about the body's response to fear is that it is exactly the same for an imagined fear as it is for an actual fear of something right in front of you in the material world.

If you are in the African Savanna and you see a lion, your body responds the same whether you actually see a lion or whether you just thought you saw a lion.

If you just think about that, it is amazing. Imagine you are sitting at home staring blankly out the window. Suddenly just a single thought can pop into your head. Depending on the thought, a feeling of sadness or euphoria or lustfulness or anger can sweep through your body in an instant. Your pancreas secretes a hormone and your liver makes an enzyme that wasn't there just moments before. The blood flow around your body is altered.

And what was the cause of all these physiological changes? A single thought in your mind that doesn't exist anywhere except right there, and only then for a fleeting second.

Bruce Lipton talks about the effects of fear on the body and its ability to perform in a state of stress in his series on Conscious Parenting.

He discusses the three key things that happen when we are in a state of fear:

First, the cells of the body move from growth into protection. Blood moves from the viscera at the core of the body out to the extremities (muscles of the arms and legs) in order to engage in fight or to get ready for flight.

Second, the immune system shuts down because there is no point using energy fighting a virus that may kill you in ten days if this lion could eat you in the next ten seconds.

And third, the blood moves away from the fore brain to the hind brain so that instead of reason and logic you are better able to engage in reflexive behaviors. You lose your ability to think rationally when you are stressed.

Estimates put the figure at well over 90% for the things we fear but never actually happen. I once heard worry described as chewing gum for the mind – it just gives it something to do but produces no meaningful results.

If a fear of loud noises or a fear of falling is holding you back from reaching your dreams, then you can take comfort in the fact that they've been there all along. But if it's a fear of anything else, then that's something you've picked up along the way. It's something you've learned to see in a certain way and that means it's something you can unlearn and relearn in a more helpful and healthy way.

Put another way, there are beliefs about the world that you have acquired throughout your life. These beliefs are responsible for the emotions you experience in your body in response to events in the outside world (and your inside world). The feelings you experience in that marvelous body of yours, like doubt, fear and anxiety, stop you from doing things that you would otherwise like to do. If any of these things are stopping you from achieving your goals and dreams, then the underlying beliefs that are responsible need to go!

"The way we communicate with others and with ourselves ultimately determines the quality of our lives"

~ Anthony Robbins

ACTION EXERCISES

What are you most afraid of?

What are four other things that you are afraid of?

Are any of these five fears holding you back from what you want to achieve?

What would change in your life if you could overcome one or more of these fear?

Write out the answers, or think about them, or better yet, discuss them with a loved one.

IT'S UP TO ME!

CHAPTER 6

Does Everyone See It That Way?

"Men are disturbed not by the things that happen to them, but by the views they take of them."

~ Epictetus

One of the most empowering exercises I have ever been a part of was called the *One*

Hundred People Technique. It is a simple exercise, but extremely powerful experientially.

For example, if I were working on an issue with my business partner this is what it would look like.

First of all, I would describe the problem in a little detail and described how I felt, the emotion that I experienced in the face of this problem. My partner would then ask me to imagine one hundred people, very similar to myself, who were facing the same challenge. "Would they all respond in the same way as you?" she asks. I'd think about the question very briefly and say something like, "Yes. Of course they would, because that's the proper response to this type of challenge. Everyone would respond the same way, wouldn't they?"

She would answer with another question, "Well, what might some of the other possible ways of responding be?"

Eventually, and somewhat reluctantly, I would have to admit that some people may be even more angry and offended than I was.

She would then say, "Good! And what about some of the others?"

"Well, I guess some others might not be really bothered by this sort of thing."

"Good!" she'd say again, "What about some other responses?" After a few minutes of this I would more than likely came up with many different possible responses —anger, laughter, indifference, offended, pleased, scornful, sarcastic, guilty, etc.

She would then say, "And do you really believe that some people may respond in these different ways?"

And I would genuinely believe that they could.

Then she would say, "Well, can you see then, that if it is possible for different people to respond in different ways to the same event, it can't be the event that is responsible for the feeling. It must be something else. It must be the individual!"

This is a critical point for most people because not only do they really accept, for the first time, that it was something in them that was creating the emotions, but they also would realize (at least I did anyway) that they only got to that realization by actually doing the exercise.

"We are disturbed, not by the events of life, but by the views we take of them."

~ Epictetus

Don't let the simplicity of this example fool you. You see, I had heard the exercise explained by the lecturer several times. And I understood it, but I didn't really get it. It was only when I took part in the exercise myself and actually came face to face with what I believed at a subconscious level that I realized it was what was inside of me that was causing the problem, not something outside of me. It wasn't them at all. It was me.

It is a powerful realization indeed when you understand that your beliefs are the key to your emotions. It is what you believe about the event that causes the emotion, not the event itself.

The way you see the world also comes from what you believe. Your perception of the world is a consequence of your acquired beliefs. And your beliefs are the result of a learning process, not a reflection of reality.

Some people see a situation a certain way and they feel they only have one real option of how to proceed. As a result of this belief, they keep banging their head against the same wall, over and over again, going round and round in circles, getting the same results.

But other people see the same situation differently. They perceive a number of different options. They make different choices and they never experience the same challenges that the other person is stuck with.

"Choice is a function of awareness."

~ Michael Beckwith

I believe Michael Beckwith from Agape Church in Los Angeles, said it best when he said "choice is a function of awareness."

The more aware you are, the more options you perceive in any given situation. The more options you are aware of, the higher the likelihood of picking the best option for you in that particular set of circumstances.

This is especially true in relationships. If you allow yourself to continually respond in the same way because you think you are right, then it can perpetuate the same vicious disagreements. You go round and round in angry circles, sometimes for years.

It is not uncommon for people to cling to their sense of rightness, even long after the other party has passed away. The same emotions of anger or resentment rise up at the mere thought of the disagreement.

If you can find another way of seeing this —if you can search for other ways to respond— you will eventually bring about a different, better, more healthy end result.

And while it may be true that the obligation sits equally with both parties in the relationship, if one just cannot see things differently at this time, and the other can, then the one with the greater awareness has the responsibility for moving things forward.

There is a lovely scene in the movie, Night at the Museum when Ben Stiller's character is hitting the monkey in the face, and the monkey is hitting him back. And on and on it goes for some time. Up rides Teddy Roosevelt on his horse and says, "Larry, why are you hitting the monkey?" He says, "He started it!" And Teddy replies, "Larry, who's evolved?"

The responsibility sits with the person with the higher awareness.

"Don't bother trying to change the world, the world you see doesn't even exist."

~ Ramana Maharshi

Ramana Maharshi was an Indian mystic who reportedly reached enlightenment at a young age. He said that there are no levels of reality, only levels of experience of the individual. That's a neat way of putting it, isn't it?

He also said of people intent on "saving the world" or changing the world, "Don't bother trying to change the world because the world you see doesn't even exist."

Paul Martinelli was one of the first people I heard talking about the idea of awareness. The more I think about it, the more I think it is the answer to everything.

So how do we gain a higher level of awareness? From experience. But not simply from experience. Everyone gets experience but not everyone grows at the same rate do they? The experience must be evaluated in some way and insight needs to be harvested from the experience. That insight needs to lead to change in the way we see the world and how we operate in it.

So you could say that intention mixed with continually evaluated experience leads to a greater level of awareness over time.

"If I had a dollar for every time I got distracted man I'd love some ice cream   right now."

~ Unknown

ACTION EXERCISES

What is holding you back from taking the next step toward your goal or your dream?

What other options can you identify rather than not moving forward?

Write out five different actions you could take, irrespective of whether or not you think they will work?

Is there anyone you know who could deal with this differently? If so, what would they do?

Write out the answers, or think about them, or better yet, discuss them with a loved one.

IT'S UP TO ME!

CHAPTER 7

ARE YOU MILKING THIS?

"Every action has its pleasures and its price."

~ Socrates

When my brother Philip (or Phil as he preferred to be called) was very young my parents began to notice that he wasn't like all the rest of us kids. To cut a long story short, after several misdiagnoses, Phil was finally diagnosed with Muscular Dystrophy or MD for short.   MD refers to the group of genetic diseases characterized by progressive weakness and degeneration of the skeletal muscles that control movement.   MD can lead to mobility impairment or even paralysis and eventually death.

For what seemed like weeks, my parents were beside themselves, not knowing really what to do or how they should react.

Why didn't my parents spend this time thinking about and enjoying the time they had with Phil? Well, certainly part of it had to do with adjusting to a new reality from the position of my parent's expectations for his future.   And that takes time.   It's like Susan Galbraith once said "Once you stop worrying about what you haven't got, you can start enjoying what you have."

But then there's another aspect to it. I call it the "poor me" syndrome. This syndrome occurs during the moment when we first realize there is a definite benefit to sharing the story of how unfortunate we have been in order to receive attention and sympathy. Being a victim can have good payoffs, after all. It also excuses you from the effort of trying, doesn't it?

Of course, if you had shared this truth with my parents at the time they would have reacted quite angrily, I'm sure. Nevertheless, it must be acknowledged that there are often benefits to us in our proclaimed misery.

I remember hearing a story about a hypnotherapist who was working with one of her clients who was being treated for migraines. She asked the client, "What happens when you get one of your headaches?"

She explained the awful experience. "Well, I have to go to bed and shut the curtains because I need absolute quiet. My husband has to come home early and feed the kids. He has to do their homework with them, make dinner, bathe them and put them to bed. I'm unable to help in any way because I have to lie down and rest."

While I certainly don't want to offend people who suffer with migraines or any other type of similar conditions, is it possible that there are significant secondary gains with many of our complaints?

I read in a book once about a psychoanalyst who said whenever anyone first explains their problems to him, the very first question he asks himself is how convenient is this? In other words, what are you getting out of this?

Dr. David Hawkins recommended putting a sign up on the mirror where you could see it every morning that reads "Yours is the saddest story I've ever heard!"

There are two types of people in the world, aren't there? There are life giving people and life draining people. Life giving people add value. They leave you a little bit better than you were when they found you. They tend to see the world from your perspective with you.

We don't seduce people by telling them how great we are; we seduce them by telling them how great they are.

You may have heard the story of the lady who went to dinner with Mr. Gladstone one evening and Mr. Disraeli the next, both prominent English Statesman.

She said, "After dinner with Mr. Gladstone I thought he was the smartest person in England; but after dinner with Mr. Disraeli I thought I was!"

What a difference between the two! Life giving people make you feel better about yourself, but they also make you feel better about the world and everyone in it. They seem to lift everything and leave you with hope. You always feel better leaving the company of a life giving person.

Life draining people, on the other hand, tend to talk about themselves and they see the world from their perspective. You always feel worse when leaving the company of life draining people!

Most of us are not aware of our real motivations. A wealthy person can work hard, make money and declare that she is doing it for the family. But the family never sees her, and when they do she seems angry and they feel like they can't live up to her high expectations. They feel like a disappointment to her. Is she really doing it for the family? Is it possible there are hidden motives? She loves the attention and the respect. Maybe she enjoys not having to look after her own children.

On the other side of the coin, a person could be without a job and because of a lack of finances, they might be forced to live on state benefits. Suffering at home all day, not enough money for a fancy car or expensive clothes or holidays to exotic places. But how convenient could that be?

If you don't have a job, you don't have to go in every day!

Of course these are simple examples not meant to be illustrative of EVERYONE in those situations, but it is certainly true that the truth is seldom in the appearance of things. In order to move up and move on, we have to let go. If you are going to be mentally and emotionally healthy, you need to let go of the opportunities you have to continually seek pity and sympathy from everyone you meet! If you really want to have a great family life, you need to make it a priority and stop doing all the other things that prevent you from sharing experiences and making memories with your family. If you really want a job, you need to let go of all the upsides of not working and spend your time learning how to become a better job candidate.

Some of you, as you read through this chapter, will be offended at the mere suggestion that your misery has any upside whatsoever. How horrible of me to even come up with such an outlandish idea! And then you will seek out people to validate your feelings. You'll tell them how offended you are. And you will explain again just how awful your lot in life is. Once again you will soak up whatever sympathy is available. Paul Martinelli describes the tendency of people to look for opportunities to be offended as one of the "four pillars of drama" in his incredible teachings. Why would anyone possibly look to be offended? Simply because there is something in it for them.

Perhaps this is why Socrates said "know thyself." The unexamined life is not worth living. If you are really honest with yourself, how convenient are your challenges? Are you prepared to give up these conveniences in order to move forward with your life?

"Try to leave out the bit readers tend to skip!"

~ Elmore Leonard

ACTION EXERCISES

Where are you stuck in your life?

Are there any upsides to being stuck?

What would someone who knows you well say is the reason you are not moving on?

Do you know anyone who is stuck in a key area of their life, who you know has significant advantages from staying stuck?

Write out the answers, or think about them, or better yet, discuss them with a loved one.

IT'S UP TO ME!

CHAPTER 8

YOU ARE PERFECT JUST AS YOU ARE!

"Be kind for everyone you meet is fighting a hard battle."

~ Socrates

I am sitting in Costa Rica looking out of a hotel window as I write this chapter. I am are here with over 250 John Maxwell Team coaches at the invitation of the president, to bring leadership transformation to this beautiful country. I have been very lucky to have the opportunity to travel extensively, working with people from over 70 different countries around the world, and one of the things that has become so obvious to me is this —the more people you meet, everyone is different, yet everyone is the same!

"The only good is knowledge and the only evil is ignorance."

~ Socrates

I believe we are all perfectly imperfect children of God, and no matter where you go or who you speak to, everyone is stepping forward courageously to face the human condition. One of my mentors said, "Having the courage to say yes to life is an incredible thing." The courage of a mother to risk her life to give birth to another life. The courage of a father to stand up to protect his family, his country, his way of life. The courage of every single one of us to stand up and say yes to our life experience. Life is good!

We are not all meant to be star quarterbacks, nor beauty pageant queens. We are not all meant to be presidents of countries or Mother Teresas.

Every single one of us is different. And every single one of us is perfect. Each one struggles in some area of life and every single one of us is loved unconditionally.

If you look around, you see people doing their best. Everyone is doing the best they can. Socrates said man always chooses the good.

Man can only choose the good. His only error is that he does not know what is for his own good. Everyone makes the best decision they can at the time.

This simple message has been said time and time again throughout history, "The only sin is ignorance."

If we accept the fact that we do what we do because we don't know better, then our path becomes pretty straightforward, doesn't it? How can we learn more and grow more so that we can make better decisions? How can we be just a little more enlightened?

Paul Martinelli often says, "The perfect curriculum for your growth is whatever lies in front of you right now."

I find this a very empowering train of thought.

- We are all perfectly imperfect.

- No one is any better than anyone else.

- No one is any worse than anyone else.

- We are all doing the best we can.

- We can all do better.

- We all have the opportunity to learn and grow.

- As we learn and grow we make better decisions.

- As we make better decisions our life improves.

- As our lives improve the lives of the people around us improve.

Isn't it nice to think that we are ALL doing the best we can? It certainly makes pride seem pretty empty and forgiveness much more of a rational decision. *Forgive us our trespasses as we forgive those that trespass against us.*

We are all in it together...and we are all connected.

There is a story about the word Ubuntu, which, to a certain African tribe means, "I am what I am because of who we all are."

It is said that an anthropologist who was studying the customs and lifestyle of this tribe spent a lot of time with the children. One particular day he decided to play a game with them. He knew they loved candy, so he made a trip to a neighboring town to buy some. He arranged quite a few pieces in a decorative basket and placed the prize at the base of a tree.

Excitedly, he called all the children together explaining that they were going to play a game and the winner would receive the prize, "When I shout "now", everyone will run as fast as you can to the tree! The first one there wins the entire basket of candy."

Eager to participate, the children lined up and waited for the shout. As soon as the anthropologist yelled, "Now!" all the children grabbed each other by the hand and began running as fast as they could toward the tree. Arriving at exactly the same time, they divided the candy and began to enjoy their prize.

Slightly stunned, the anthropologist asked why they chose to all run together when the winner would have had all the candy to themselves.

"Ubuntu. How could one of us be happy when the others are sad?"

This philosophy and way of life speaks about our interconnectedness. You can't exist as a human all by yourself. Our choices affect others. Every day we have crossroads and decisions...With each decision we either choose to add value to another human life or to take it away. We are always choosing one or the other. Even the decision to do nothing, is still a decision.

Part of walking in awareness is understanding that we are responsible for the condition we leave others in. How has their encounter with us affected them? What lasting impression have I left?

We often talk about leaving a legacy for future generations. Often we are referring to finances or inheritance, but what about our daily legacy? We are building a memorial to ourselves with every sentence, every text message, every email, every glance.

Realizing this certainly changes our perspective, doesn't it?

"These are my principles. If you don't like them, I have others."

~ **Groucho Marx**

ACTION EXERCISES

What aspects of you are you not happy with?

How do they affect your life?

Do you know anyone who has similar things that is not bothered by them at all or uses them as an advantage?

How could it be true that your weaknesses are also your sensitivities?

Write out the answers, or think about them, or better yet, discuss them with a loved one.

IT'S UP TO ME!

CHAPTER 9

LOVE ALL LIFE, INCLUDING YOURSELF!

"A fear of weakness only strengthens weakness."

– Criss Jami

You have flaws. I have flaws. We are not perfect. We're all going to make mistakes. It's simply part of the human process.

Shocking, right?

Actually, I'm quite certain you didn't flinch at all when you read those words. Isn't it amazing that although we are fully aware of the fact that mistakes, detours and unexpected results are part of the process, we often allow the fear of their arrival to stall our progress? Some of us get stuck for days or weeks, while others struggle with the fear of failure to such a degree that it can derail our dreams indefinitely.

But why? Why do we get stuck?

In the closing chapters of Think and Grow Rich, Napoleon Hill uncovers the six basic fears that prevent us from attaining freedom and success:

- The fear of poverty.

- The fear of criticism.

- The fear of ill health.

- The fear of losing someone.

- The fear of old age.

- The fear of death.

These are core fears. As we talked about earlier, they are learned. Depending on how we were raised or what we've experienced, these fears can affect us to a greater or lesser degree.

How do we combat fear? How do we push past the irrational and negative thought patterns that trigger survival mode and constrict the hope around us?

How do we live struggle free?

The good news here is, there is a way to retrain your brain. It doesn't matter if you're eighteen or eighty, the negative thoughts that run through your brain can be recognized, rejected and replaced.

Let's take a look at how that's accomplished:

Fear is connected to our lens. It has to do with how we see things, and especially, how we see ourselves. For the most part, we see situations through our own filter or according to certain expectations. We do this automatically, or without really thinking about it.

For example, let's say five or six of us were discussing real estate investing during dinner...

The deeper a few of us got into the conversation, the more you checked-out and disengaged.

Why? Because you're not an investor.

Not only do you not invest in real estate, but you've never owned a home in your life. In fact, your parents never owned a home either. So, instead of leaning in (which would be alignment), you might choose to lean away. It probably wasn't even a conscious decision. You see, the left side of our brain (the part that's linear and rational) is constantly taking information from our experiences and connecting this information to our current reality in order to project probable outcomes. So, if the entire table is talking about investing and you don't believe that's something attainable for you, it's likely the left side of your brain made the probable assumption that you'll never need this information, so go ahead and check-out.

Hold it right there!

What if investing becomes somehow connected to your future success? What if you're a late bloomer but buying property is now vital to your life? Well, once you have this awareness (become awake to this truth) you have the power to change, to learn, to grow.

Maybe you'll have to overcome some of the core fears Napoleon Hill discussed. Fear robs us of our power. While we are saying yes to our dreams and goals, fear is saying no.

Instead of allowing these fears to run around in our brain like a wild banshee, it's up to us to

- **RECOGNIZE** The Fears

- **REJECT** The Fears and

- **REPLACE** The Fears

It's like being the bouncer of your own brain. If there are negative thoughts and limiting belief systems in there, it's our job to kick them out. Limiting beliefs are beliefs developed during our life which limit our ability to reach our full potential. For example, when I was told in Elementary School that I had a reading disability. From that point forward, I developed a limiting belief system that told me I was dumb and stupid and would never amount to anything. Because of this, when things started to go right in my life, without even being aware of it, I would do something stupid to sabotage my own success in order to stay in alignment with my own limiting belief system.

Let's go one level deeper and talk about how we kick negative thoughts out. It's certainly not by using willpower and choosing not to think negative thoughts. If you've ever attempted to not think about something, you know how well that works.

If you've never tried it, go ahead and spend the next thirty seconds trying not to picture a purple zebra. Don't do it! No purple zebras!

Let me guess ... they're galloping around in your brain at full speed, right? I thought so.

Instead of attempting to not think negatively, the key is to replace fear and negative thoughts. We do this by reminding ourselves of who we are, what we're made of, and what's available to us.

You can use any positive affirmations you choose. The only requirement is that you believe what you're reading or declaring over yourself.

Simple Bible Scriptures can be very useful. They can act as your Daily Promises.

Here are a few:

"Everything I put my hand to will prosper." — Psalm 1:3

"I am fully equipped and limitlessly resourced for everything I will face today." —Hebrews 13:21

"I won't drift off my course, because the Word promises I will hear a voice behind me saying, 'This is the direction to walk'." —Isaiah 30:21

These are just a few, but you get the point. Replace the lies fear is trying to tell you with the truth of who you really are! When your thought-life is centered around faith and truth, you become a living, breathing container of hope. You actually begin to operate on a higher vibrational level (level of awareness). You begin to attract the things you desire because you aren't allowing any interference from fear!

I believe it's possible to form the habit of walking free from fear. It may take some practice, but the ability to boldly embrace who we are and live an authentic, courageous life is possible.

Remember, failure isn't fatal, and it certainly isn't final.

So go ahead and try! Whether you fail or not, at least you are busy with living instead of standing on the side-lines of life, and that's something to be applauded!

In 2012, Sara Blakely became the youngest self-made billionaire. She was 41. She is the creator and founder of Spanx, a women's apparel product. The thing that impressed me most about her story was her recollection of sitting around the dinner table with her father every evening. He taught her the power of failing big, and failing often. "Every evening he would ask me, 'So, what did you fail at today?' And if there were no failures, Dad would be disappointed."

Lack of failure means you are not stretching yourself outside your comfort zone.

By focusing on failing often, and using it as a freeing and liberating exercise in the process of becoming, Sara was allowed to understand that a lack of failure actually signified that she was not stretching herself far enough out of her comfort zone.

Each day we should strive to fully embrace life, and all the mess that it may bring. It's when we live to be more than we were yesterday, and chase after it without fear, that we can begin to discover what we are made of and what we can become!

As my friend and mentor Paul Martinelli likes to say, "You must jump and build your wings on the way down." John Lennon once said "There are two basic motivating forces; fear and love. When we are afraid, we pull back from life. When we love, we open to all that life has to offer with passion, excitement, and acceptance. We need to learn to love ourselves first, in all our glory and imperfections. If we cannot love ourselves, we cannot fully open our ability to love others or our potential to create."

I encourage you to take risks, push against the imaginary barriers of life. Swim in the deep end! Choose to free fall! Don't worry about failing. If you fail, it's really okay! You'll get up. You'll try again! You'll make it!

"It took me 15 years to work out I had no talent for writing, but I couldn't give it up because by then I was too famous."

~ Robert Benchley

ACTION EXERCISES

Who do you need to forgive?

Why don't you forgive them?

Where have you made mistakes in your own life?

Why is it so hard for you to forgive yourself?

What would it feel like to genuinely forgive yourself?

Write out the answers, or think about them, or better yet, discuss them with a loved one.

IT'S UP TO ME!

CHAPTER 10

IF IT'S WORTH HAVING IT'S HARD TO GET!

"I can sum up the success of my life in seven words.   Never give up.   Never, never give up."

~ Winston Churchill

The spark is fun, isn't it? It's that moment of creation when you give permission to a dream or a goal. That spark is usually accompanied by feelings of determination, optimism, passion and motivation.

Beginnings are exciting and energizing. They have the freshness of a blank page, and for most people a new endeavor can be almost intoxicating. It's kind of like the honeymoon phase of a relationship. And just like romantic relationships, substance isn't built in the beginning. It's during the trials and the day-to-day encounters with each other that "who we are inside" is established. It's when we are faced with difficult choices, challenges, trials and frustrations that we become.

During this process of becoming, our dreams are either being fulfilled or forgotten. It happens one choice at a time, because it is the process that builds us into who we really are.

Success is developed daily, not in a day.

Look around at your life. Think about your relationships, finances, and career. Now go deeper. Think about the things you're proud of, the things you've settled for, the things you'd like to change.

Everything around you is a manifestation of your daily choices. You are in current, active possession of the kingdom you've created for yourself. Good or bad. Like it or not, you are the product of your choices.

The more I meditate on this, the more I realize that there is an art to living out our passion. It is an ebb and flow, a process of constant evolving and adapting.

If you aren't happy with what you currently have, the answer then, is to begin to lean in to the choices that say yes to the fulfillment of your dreams and goals. In order to accomplish this, there really is a leveling of pride that takes place. In order to grow and become all you can be, you'll need to first take responsibility for who and WHERE you are.

Nothing good was ever born out of excuses, so if you've ever said things like, "This is how I was raised." or "I can't help it. I'm just doing what I know." I want to challenge you to absolutely ban these excuses from your life. You don't have to remain comfortable with terrible circumstances. You can take the sign off of your bathroom mirror because yours doesn't have to be the saddest story ever, but it's up to you to make that decision. Living your best life is your own choice.

As I shared in my book *Lead Bold – Lead Strong – Lead Well: 9 Proven Leadership Secrets Anyone Can Learn and Apply*, I had decided when I was ten years old I was going into the Air Force. My dream was to be a pilot. Not just any pilot, I was going to be a pilot in their premier aerial demonstration squadron, the Thunderbirds. Unfortunately, as I had stated earlier, in Elementary School, I was told I had a reading disability and from that point on I believed that I simply wasn't smart enough to ever make this dream become a reality. In fact, "I'm not smart enough" became a central theme in my life. To make a long story short, it took me many years and a seemingly endless number of mistakes to figure out just how untrue that statement was.

It is one of the most liberating things you will ever do. To stand on the wreckage heap of your own broken promises, unfulfilled commitments, lies, masks, failures and mistakes and place your signature of ownership on the whole mess; that's huge. It gives you a starting point, a place of accountability where you can say, "Yes, I'm responsible for all of that, and now I'm going to be responsible for all of this!"

Doing that is better than skydiving for the first time. It's risky, dangerous, wildly vulnerable, and 100% necessary if things are ever going to be any different in your life. Best of all, it's empowering.

We are who we choose to be. Every day. Every moment.

We don't have to wait until church on Sunday or even tomorrow morning. We literally have the power to walk in foolishness one minute and turn our entire life around the next. As soon as we realize we are doing something that's not in alignment with our best life, we have the power to choose to turn around. That decision can be made in an instant.

Right now. Or right now. Or right now.

Any moment is the right moment to adjust your alignment. And once you decide, you give permission once again to the fulfillment of your dream, your goal and your purpose.

And how do my tiny choices have anything to do with what level of success I'm able to attain (and maintain) in my life?

I'm glad you asked.

"Champions don't become champions in the ring, they are merely recognized there." ~ John C. Maxwell

Success is merely the evidence of the level of discipline and commitment you've held up. It's just like physical muscles are proof of your commitment to work out every day.

Star athletes don't become champions on the field. They are merely recognized there. They became a champion every time they said yes to their dream, got up early, finished their workout routine, and did what others were not willing to do in order to better themselves. Your success or failure is hidden in your daily routine. That's where it all happens. If you cheat there, it will come out eventually.

Former heavyweight champion, Joe Frazier, said, "You can map out a fight plan, but when the action starts, it boils down to reflexes. That's where your road work shows. If you've cheated on that in the dark of the morning, you'll get found out under the bright lights."

This is a perfect analogy for success in every area of our lives. It's all about what you do when no one is watching. It's about what you do to prepare. Do you walk in excellence? Do you operate in integrity? Are all your choices bringing you closer to the fulfillment of your dream?

Okay, now let's go back to the chapter title, "If it's worth having, it's hard to get."

This statement is both true and untrue at the same time. The bottom line is this; any choice you make has "hard" attached to it:

- Choice #1: If you choose to live with intention and fulfill your destiny, it will be hard. Things will come against you. You'll often have to go against the status-quo. You may feel lonely at times and without encouragement. You'll need self-discipline, commitment, and to constantly remind yourself that you can do this. You'll have to give yourself pep-talks and learn how to quickly realign yourself when you start to drift off course. Are all these things hard? Absolutely!

- Choice #2: If you choose to slack off, settle for less than you are capable of or become complacent, it will be hard. You'll constantly wonder what you could have achieved if you had only changed your habits and said yes to your dreams. You'll regret the fact that you never stepped out of your comfort zone long enough to experience the thrill of success. It will be hard to look at your life one day and wonder what you could have been, if only you would have given yourself permission.

If you look at it this way, I'm sure you'll agree that both choices are hard. It's just that one comes with the promise of a fulfilled life and the ability to walk in freedom, while the other comes with disappointment and regret.

Both paths are hard.

My advice to you?

Choose *your* hard.

"The greatest oak was once just a little nut who held its ground."

~ Anonymous

ACTION EXERCISES

What is the difference between being stubborn and being committed?

When you give up on something, how do you explain it to yourself? Do you identify good reasons why you are stopping?

What is the upside of giving up in these areas?

What is the downside of giving up in these areas?

Write out the answers, or think about them, or better yet, discuss them with a loved one.

IT'S UP TO ME!

CHAPTER 11

WHERE IS MY WHY?

"The two most important days of your life are the day you were born, and the day you find out why."

~ Mark Twain

Each one of us was created with a purpose. There is an internal version of yourself, fully equipped with unique gifts, talents, and passions. This true version of yourself can either be suppressed, starved and ignored or nurtured and given the freedom to grow. The choice is yours.

You're not a carbon copy of anyone else. If you were, you'd be dispensable. Anyone could fill your shoes and your purpose in life. But they absolutely cannot.

We complicate things, don't we? I think the fact that we are thinking and reasoning adults is sometimes our downfall, especially when it comes to finding our "why." We start out as children filled with wonder and optimism. Children say things like, "I want to fly. I want to touch the stars. I want to live under water." Their sense of having the ability to become whatever they want has no boundaries. Limitations are learned later in life. As parents, it's our job to nurture our children's dreams and encourage them to follow their natural bent (talent or inclination). There are numerous childhood development studies that outline the benefits of allowing your child to search, explore and follow their dreams.

The Bible provides some awe-inspiring insight into this way of thinking. Proverbs 18:16 assures us, "A man's gifts will make room for him."

Your gift is that divine spark that you were born with. It is that certain something you were created to live out and be. Your gift is connected to your purpose, your passion and ultimately, your ability to live a fulfilled life. It is all wrapped up in your big "why."

When you're operating in your gift and walking out your purpose, it doesn't matter how difficult the journey is. It doesn't matter how much time it takes to evolve or become exactly what you are called to be. Money, education, and time invested in your purpose doesn't feel like a sacrifice to you, because it's what you are meant to do! There is an inner passion connected to our purpose!

German philosopher Friedrich Nietzsche said, "He who has a why to live for can bear almost any how."

How long? How difficult? How much will it cost me? How far will I have to go? How much more will I have to learn? How many more obstacles will I face? These things don't matter when you have your "why!"

It's interesting to take note of the fact that the Scripture doesn't say, "Your education will make room for you." Now, I fully believe in educating yourself, but if education alone was the secret to a fulfilled life, then everyone with a degree would be living out the best version of themselves. Today's statistics on career fulfillment prove otherwise. Gallup surveys show that over 60% of the working population across all career tracks, educational levels and industries are "not engaged" or are "actively disengaged" from their work. It's not that we, as a whole, have lost our ability to connect with meaningful work. I believe the answer to this disengagement is the fact that most of us are not living out our purpose. The work we are doing might be meaningful to the right person, but not to us!

When we actively suppress the part of our being that wants to dream and grow, and instead, force ourselves onto paths that we imagine to be less risky or more practical, we are settling for a life we were never meant to live. You can have all the education in the world, but if you're not actively reaching toward your individual life purpose, something will always feel "off." It is that unsatisfied gnawing that many of us can't put our finger on.

The good news here is that your "why" is right where you left it and you can pick it up at any moment. You have an internal compass that can still be accessed. It's the place where your dreams are still alive.

So, the question then is, "Where is my why and how do I find it?"

Your journey to your "why" truly begins when you make that first decision in awareness. The moment you say to yourself, "I will give myself permission to find and live out my life purpose," the entire universe conspires together to bring it to pass. You move from darkness to light by one choice. The follow-up actions and steps you will take will reveal themselves along the way.

It begins with the decision to actively disengage from everyone else's expectations and allow yourself to fully access that inner child who was allowed to dream big.

Think about it. Do you remember the last time you woke up with a true sense of purpose, or have you been operating as a slave to the deadlines and constant flood of distractions offered up by the influences around you? Remember, in an earlier chapter you learned that you have to be the bouncer of your own brain. It goes deeper than just focusing on positive thoughts and believing in yourself. You also have to agree to protect the vision and purpose that you've been given, even if it hasn't fully revealed itself yet.

It's as simple as this: The key to walking is to continue to walk. Once you decide to live out your purpose, you will naturally find yourself in positions where you will have opportunities to choose to nurture your dreams. You will also have opportunities to suppress them. It is a continual choice you are making with every step.

"But how will I know?"

This is where most people get stuck. Many of us aren't used to accessing our internal compass. It seems too New Age to nurture an unknown path. "What if I make a mistake? What if I fail?" See the vicious cycle? That kind of thinking will have you right back in the grip of fear. Fear of the unknown is what keeps us in the bondage of settling for far less than we were created to be.

The truth is, you don't have to know exactly how it will all come together, and I can promise you that you won't! Your biggest responsibility in this process of becoming is to choose to say yes to your purpose every day without putting a cap on your dreams.

Everything else will come to you. Why? Because as you begin to say yes to your true purpose and give yourself permission to live free from the prison you've put yourself in, you will begin to see your goals and dreams with ever increasing clarity. The fact that you want to see them is all it takes for them to begin to appear. The more you say yes, the more will be revealed. You've only been stuck all this time because you made a decision to leave your dreams and goals behind. You lost your "why" when you traded your purpose for something that seemed easier or more secure.

Compromise will always be offered up to you, so get used to that. But as you continue to live a life intent on fulfilling your purpose, the voices of the things you used to settle for will begin to sound more ridiculous.

It's like the guy who pushed against all odds to become the first entrepreneur in his family. He started out cutting his neighbor's lawn, and now ten years later he has seven crews who are responsible for all the golf-course properties in his town. What would happen if someone walked up to him and offered him a secure management job with an hourly pay rate? If entrepreneurship is connected to his "why" and he is living out his purpose, he would laugh at that offer. Sure, it may seem like less work, less responsibility and a guaranteed paycheck, but in reality this man's passion is already attached to his business.

He is fulfilled. He is continuing to grow. In fact, he just provided two jobs last month to young men who are in the community re-entry program. These men served time in jail and now are receiving a second chance at life. This extra layer of fulfillment further connects this entrepreneur to his "why." Do you think he knew he'd be helping change lives when he first felt that inner pull to start his own lawn service company? Of course not, but he had the courage to follow his inner compass. He decided to say yes to that pull.

Where is your inner compass pointing you? If you choose to listen and continue to give yourself permission to live out your greatest purpose, you will find it, because it's already within you.

What is your WHY?

*"Good judgement comes from experience.
Experience comes from bad judgement."*

~ **Will Rogers**

ACTION EXERCISES

Do you know why you are here?

Are you happy to not know why you are here?

Do you know anyone who passionately pursues their purpose?

What difference does it make in their life?

If you don't know your purpose, are you spending some time every day looking for it?

Write out the answers, or think about them, or better yet, discuss them with a loved one.

IT'S UP TO ME!

CHAPTER 12

SUMMARY

"God doesn't require us to succeed; He only requires that you try."

~ Mother Teresa

If you've got this far through the book, I'm guessing you're ready for the next marvelous chapter of your life. It's time for a change, right? Another ten years on autopilot is just not an option any more.

I used to lay in bed thinking to myself, "I wonder what I'm capable of if I really threw myself into something with all my might?"

And it was a comforting thought for a while. It took me away from the humdrum of my daily, disappointing existence; but inevitably I had to return at some point.

The interesting thing was that I somehow thought that the only requirement for my dream life to unfold was for me to be discovered, that someone would spot my genius and then everything would be alright! How can you delude yourself to that extent?

Eventually I came to the realization that nothing is going to happen unless I make it happen. No one is going to discover you, no one is going to make it easy for you, no one is going to take away the pain. You have to do it for yourself.

For some people that might be bad news. But when you think about it, it means that your new life can begin any moment you choose. You are not waiting for anyone.

Your life may be dark and disappointing, but hope begins in the dark.

You may be worried about failing. You may be concerned about being disappointed if things don't work out as you want it to. Well, you will be disappointed, because you will fail. But failure is temporary if you keep going. And what's the alternative? You are certainly doomed if you don't even try.

You may be worried about what other people will say. And it's true, you may well be in for ridicule and criticism from those who lack your courage not to settle for a stagnant life. But those who never made a mistake never tried anything new. And there is only one way to avoid criticism: do nothing, say nothing, and be nothing. And it's obvious where that will lead.

You may berate yourself for not having started all this years ago, surely it's too late now. But no matter how old you are, you have the rest of your life ahead of you. It is pure folly not to go after a goal because of the amount of time it will take to achieve it, because the time is going to pass anyway!

Maybe you could have started years ago. Perhaps the very best time to begin would have been ten or even twenty years ago. But you didn't, so the second best time is right now. It's never too late to become what you could have been!

"Too many of us are not living our dreams because we are too busy living our fears."

~ **Les Brown**

Why don't more of us go for it then? My friend Les Brown says that too many of us are not living our dreams because we are living our fears. (He also said that the tiger doesn't concern himself with the opinion of the sheep, which although it doesn't fit here, I love it!)

We just can't afford to allow fear to hold us back. We have to find a way to go after our dreams, because if we don't, then we will spend our time working for someone else, building their dreams for them.

We don't need to be a genius and we don't need to be an overnight success. It doesn't matter how long it takes us or how slowly we go, as long as we don't give up. As long as we don't stop.

How we react to failure often has more to do with how we see ourselves than it does with how we see our situation.

We need to find the motivation to keep moving forward, to go from one failure to the next with no loss of enthusiasm.

The more we persist, the more we develop character. And character is ours to keep.

"You need to go out and make a mess!"

~ Roddy Galbraith

If we are going to be successful in living out our dream life, then we have to stand up straight and look life in the eye. We need to take part. We need to go out and make a mess!

Probably the happiest I've seen my children is when we walked down the road outside our house after it has been raining and watch them jump in the puddles with their little rubber boots on. The sheer delight in their faces is beyond the comprehension of the adult mind at least it is mine. They would jump in those puddles for hours if I'd let them. And when I'd drag them back in the house because they are soaked and cold, they would cry because I've ruined their experience.

How do we become so paralyzed and unadventurous in adult life? Why are we so worried about messing up, making mistakes or appearing foolish?

As my mentor John Maxwell says, no one is good at anything the first time. So if we are going to try new things, we are going to mess up.

And that's ok! That's good!

As we take part in life, we learn and grow. But I'm talking about more than just doing something different. That is change, but change is not enough. Change is doing something different but transformation is being something different.

I'm talking about being something different tomorrow than you are today.

But more than that, evolution is continual transformation, and that's what we need in our lives, continual growth.   Continual change. Continual transformation. Continual evolution.

I believe that's why we're here, to experience life and to learn and grow from our experiences. To grow physically, mentally and spiritually.

I adopted my "mission" in life from a mentor of mine several years ago – helping leaders develop leaders.

And I firmly believe that the only way any of us can do that, is by living life to the fullest – by going out and making a mess.

I believe that is our responsibility, to live. And we don't need to worry about doing it perfectly.

We are responsible for the effort, not the result.

We can't control a great deal about the world and all the other people in it, but we can control our own efforts. We can all do our best, and that's all it takes.

Good luck and may God bless you on your journey. Start now and go as far as you can see. When you get there you'll see how to go further. Discover the Real You!

IT'S UP TO ME!

THE END!

"Action comes about if and only if we find a discrepancy between what we are experiencing and what we want to experience."

~ Philip J. Runkel

Thank you for investing in yourself, buying this book and reading it! If you would like to find out more about some of our other learning resources, go to:

www.d2dleadership.com

SPECIAL THANKS!

I would like to say THANK YOU to some special people who really helped me with this book:

Lisa Hoffman

Paul Gustavson

Randy Wheeler

Roddy Galbraith

ABOUT THE AUTHOR

"When you truly believe in yourself and what you are trying to accomplish, others will believe in you and your vision as well."

~ Mike T. Lightner

Mike Lightner is a retired Chief Master Sergeant from the United States Air Force with extensive knowledge and experience in team leadership and personnel development. In his last position, as the Aircrew Flight Equipment Career Field Manager, he oversaw the leadership, growth, development and management of over 5,200 Total Force (Active Duty, Air National Guard, and Reserve Airmen, and civilian employees) worldwide. Additional, Mike was responsible for the inspection, maintenance, acquisition, and sustainment of over $8 Billion in critical life sustaining aircrew and passenger safety, survival, and chemical defense equipment.

As a John C. Maxwell Certified International Coach, Teacher, and Speaker, Mike offers workshops, seminars, keynote speaking, and coaching, designed to aid you in your personal and professional growth through study and practical application of proven leadership methods.

Mike's passion is to develop leaders who, in turn, have a passion to develop leaders. If this is the type culture you would like to create within your organization, he stands ready to help you achieve your goal!

mikelightner@d2dleadership.com

www.d2dleadership.com

87498329R00110

Made in the USA
Lexington, KY
25 April 2018